Art
SCHOOL

Mick Manning&
Brita Granström

F
FRANCES LINCOLN
CHILDREN'S BOOKS

Brita Granström – this book is for you – M.M.
Thanks! – B.G.

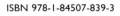

With thanks to: Chester, Terry and Sue
at Kingfisher; and all my art teachers at home,
Haworth, Hartington, Greenhead, Bradford Foundation,
Newcastle Polytechnic and The Royal College of Art
– Mick Manning

This edition published in Great Britain and in the USA in 2008 by
Frances Lincoln Children's Books, 4 Torriano Mews,
Torriano Avenue, London NW5 2RZ
www.franceslincoln.com

British Library Cataloguing in Publication Data
available on request

ISBN 978-1-84507-839-3

Printed in China

9 8 7 6 5 4 3 2 1

Contents

4 What this book is about

6 What is drawing anyway?

9 Keeping sketchbooks

10 Self portrait

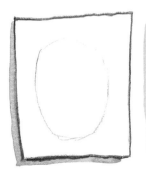  

11 Big and small... (scale)

12 Use your common senses!

16 Life drawing

18 Portrait and caricature

19 Light and shadow

20 Colour workshop

22 Still life and composition

24 Reportage

26 The artist as explorer

28 Field trip

30 Maps

32 Mail art

33 Masks

34 Sculpture

36 Frottage

37 Collage

38 Land art

40 Make your own paper

42 Book work

44 Art history

46 Show

47 Glossary

48 Certificate

4

Hi, I'm Mick Welcome to my Art School! Get ready. We're about to begin ...

When you join this Art School, you won't just learn how to draw and paint, you will also learn how to see things in new and exciting ways. You'll be able to try all kinds of projects, from experimenting with colour to making masks and sending mail art – just like one of my real art students. Keep practising, and slowly you will build up a range of different art skills.

You will need plenty of things to draw with and paint on but you don't have to spend a lot of money. See below and page 7 for ideas.

What to draw and paint on

You can buy cheap drawing **paper** from an art shop. Ask for **A2** cartridge paper or sugar paper. Or paint newspaper and old rolls of wallpaper with white **emulsion**.

What to draw and paint with

You'll need:

- Poster paint or powder paint
- Watercolours · Inks
- Wax crayons and oil pastels
- Empty yoghurt pots
- Plastic bottles to put water in
- Pencils and brushes
- Wax candle · Tape
- Glue · Paper scissors

ART SCHOOL TIPS

Look out for helpful tips in the coloured strips down the side of each page.

You can find out more about the words that appear in **bold type** in the glossary at the back of the book.

5

PROJECT

Try these different ways of holding your **pencil** or **crayon**.
1. Grip with your thumb and middle finger, resting your wrist on the paper.
2. Swing your wrist, like this.
3. Hold your pencil firmly for a hard line.
4. Move your whole arm from the shoulder down to the fingertips.
5. Press lightly for a soft line.

What is drawing anyway?

Let's begin at the beginning and think about what a drawing actually is. I would describe a drawing as a series of deliberate marks. These marks describe how someone sees something, or even what they think about something. We usually think of a drawing as a picture, but it doesn't have to be. A scribbled shopping list, a map on the back of an envelope, or even your handwriting, can all be described as drawings. Whatever a drawing is, to be able to draw really well you need to relax.

1.

3.

4.

5.

2.

6

sponge tied to a stick

sponge brush

wax crayon

oil pastel

charcoal

feather

square brush

round brush

twig or stick

pencil

steel nib

wax candle with ink or watercolour on top

old toothbrush makes nice marks

big brush

Experiment:
Use all your drawing tools and fill a large sheet of paper with as many different marks as you can.

Write the name of each tool next to its mark!

Making marks

PROJECT

Collect lots of different drawing tools, such as **brushes** and crayons, and try making some of your own.

Make your own sketchbook

PROJECT

What you need:
● 5 large sheets of cartridge paper (**A1** is a good size) ● Cotton or carpet tape ● Thick card ● Darning needle and thread ● **Glue**

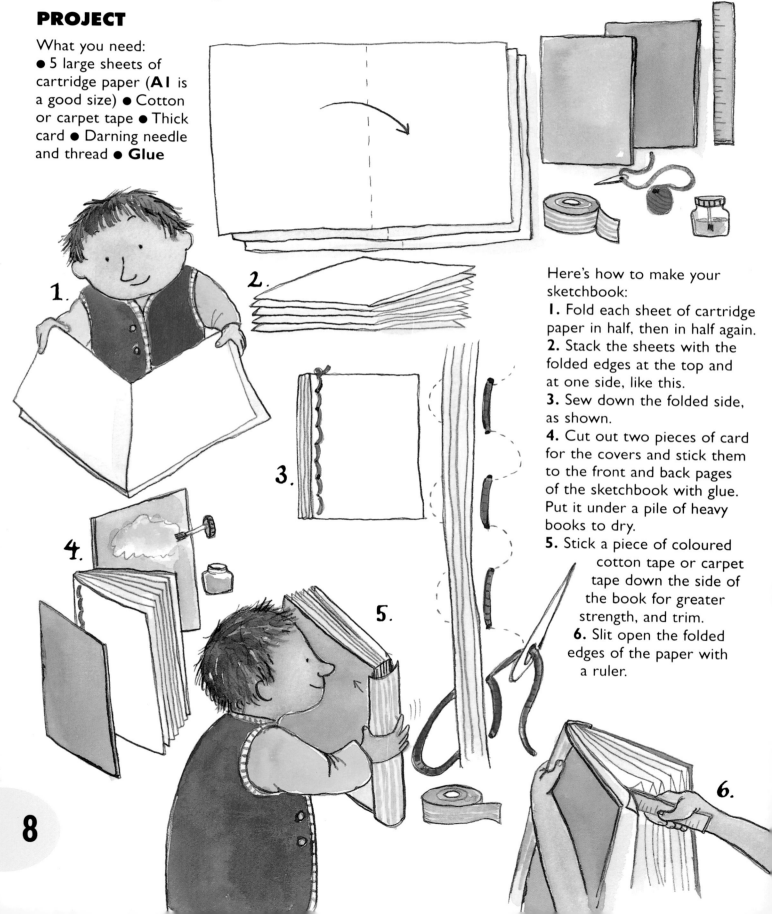

1.

2.

3.

4.

5.

6.

Here's how to make your sketchbook:

1. Fold each sheet of cartridge paper in half, then in half again.
2. Stack the sheets with the folded edges at the top and at one side, like this.
3. Sew down the folded side, as shown.
4. Cut out two pieces of card for the covers and stick them to the front and back pages of the sketchbook with glue. Put it under a pile of heavy books to dry.
5. Stick a piece of coloured cotton tape or carpet tape down the side of the book for greater strength, and trim.
6. Slit open the folded edges of the paper with a ruler.

Keeping Sketchbooks

Most artists keep a sketchbook which they carry around with them all the time. Follow the instructions on the opposite page to make your very own sketchbook, then keep it with you. Draw in it, write in it and stick things in it – anything from bus tickets to sweet wrappers. Your sketchbook should become a record of what you have seen and felt and where you have been.

Follow the instructions on the opposite page

ART SCHOOL TIPS

A pocket sketchbook is useful, too.

Landscape

Portrait

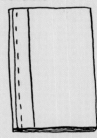

You can make your sketchbook landscape or portrait. Simply decide which edge to sew.

Keep looking backwards and forwards between your drawing and the mirror as you work, checking what you are drawing against your reflection.

10

If you rub out all the time you won't learn how to draw properly. If you're not happy with a line, try drawing over the top of it, as shown below. Keep drawing over it until it works.

Visit a library and look at the self portraits of Rembrandt and Van Gogh to see how different they are.

Self portrait

A self **portrait** is, quite simply, a picture of yourself. I want you to practise drawing your self portrait, both big and small.

PROJECT

Find a roll of old wallpaper or paint sheets of newspaper with white emulsion and stick them together. Pin the paper on the wall next to a mirror and draw yourself life-sized. This is a good way to practise doing a self portrait and using your whole arm when you draw. Next, I want you to use your imagination. Try drawing yourself as a monster. Exaggerate! Use colourful paints and make yourself as scary as possible!

Big and small... (SCALE)

Here is another project which will help you practise your drawing skills and learn about **scale**. You'll also discover how you can draw things at different sizes in different ways.

PROJECT

Find a tiny object, such as a small toy or a piece of jewellery. Study it carefully. Take a sheet of A2 cartridge paper and a black crayon or a soft pencil and draw your tiny object so big that it fills the page. Work quickly and use bold, sweeping strokes. Now choose a large object. This time I want you to draw it very, very small. As you draw, notice how only your fingers and wrist are moving.

Remember! Keep looking back and forwards between the object and your drawing.

Write down the name of
each sound as you draw it.

Try pressing down hard
for a strong smell or a
loud noise and drawing
lightly for a quiet sound
or a delicate smell.

Use your common Senses!

Most people have five senses – sight, sound, touch, taste and smell – but artists need two more – memory and imagination! Using all these senses is important for an artist because how something looks isn't everything. How it feels, smells, sounds and even tastes is also important. These projects are all about 'seeing' things with your nose, fingers, tongue and ears, not just with your eyes.

PROJECT

Wait until it is dark then go and sit in your bedroom with your crayons and paper. Switch off the light, sit quietly and listen. What can you hear? The television next door? A cat outside? Strange creaks and groans? Now pick up your crayons (it's exciting because you won't know what colours they are) and try to draw all the sounds you hear. Turn on the light to see what you've done!

Drawing in the dark

12

Drawing tastes

PROJECT

Put some food on a plate, such as a piece of apple, a slice of lemon or a biscuit. Get your paper and crayons ready, then tie a scarf around your eyes so you can't see. Now taste something from the plate. Is it sharp or sweet, sour or crunchy? Try to draw what you taste.

ART SCHOOL TIPS

It's all up to you and your imagination! Look at these black-and-white drawings and guess what they could be. See if you can match them with the small pictures in the colour illustration below.

Drawing Smells

PROJECT

Visit different places, such as your kitchen or bathroom at home, a local park or a shopping centre. Flare your nostrils and have a really good sniff, then draw what you can smell. Stinky drains, flowers, food being cooked... each has its own colour and shape.

13

Drawing textures

How something *feels* is important when you are drawing it. You wouldn't draw the same marks for a soft feather as you would for rough wood or smooth soap. Showing textures also makes your drawings look more interesting.

PROJECT

Collect several objects with different textures, for example a piece of wood with a rough grain, a scrap of tin foil, an orange, a hairbrush, a bar of soap and a feather. Try to draw how each one feels when you explore it with your fingers. It might be rough or smooth, slippery or sticky. Remember: you're not trying to draw what it *looks* like but what it *feels* like.

14

Drawing from memory

When we remember something, such as a day on the beach or a visit to the dentist, we remember the most important parts of the event as a series of memory pictures. In other words, memory can make a kind of drawing, too.

1.

2.

PROJECT

Think hard about something, such as a favourite pet. Picture it in your mind then try to draw it from memory.
Next, try a memory test:
1. Find three or four small objects and study them closely.
2. Cover them with a cloth, then draw them from memory. How did you do?

Drawing a dream

PROJECT

I want you to remember a brilliant dream you have had or a film you have watched recently. Remember as much of it as you can, then draw it step by step on the back of a long piece of wallpaper or on an A2 sheet of cartridge paper using pencils, crayons and paints. Don't use any words. Let your drawings tell the story.

ART SCHOOL TIPS

Here are some tips to help you improve your life drawing.

1. Start by looking for the shape of the skeleton underneath the skin.

2. Make a stick figure as a guide, marking out the head and body, and where the shoulders, elbows, wrists, hips, knees and ankles are.

3. Start to build up the body shape. Try to work up the whole drawing at once rather than trying to get just one part right.

4. Look for the spaces around and in between the body, too.

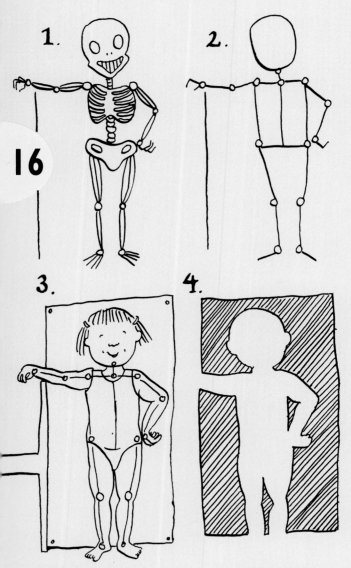

Make sure that your model is warm and comfortable before you begin. You don't want to get stuck into your drawing and find your model wants to leave!

It takes artists years and years of practice to make good life drawings, so don't be put off if you're not happy with the first ones that you do.

Life drawing

You've already tried drawing yourself. Now I want you to try life drawing – drawing somebody else! Life drawing is very important because it helps an artist learn how the human body fits together. Ask an adult or a friend to model for you wearing a swimming costume or a leotard. This helps you see the body shape easily.

When you are life drawing, it sometimes helps if you use your pencil like a measure. Hold your pencil out at arm's length and look down it with one eye shut. For example, it may be half a pencil from your model's elbow to leg and the same distance from their neck to belly button. Try to keep the same **proportions** on your drawing.

Use your imagination to create amazing action pictures!

Action and costume

PROJECT

Set up a life-drawing class with some friends and take it in turns to model. Find different costumes and use chairs and cushions to get interesting poses. Later, you can turn your life drawings into action scenes by adding imaginary backgrounds.

ART SCHOOL TIPS

When you use your pencil to measure scale, don't forget that you have to hold the pencil at the same distance from your eye every time.

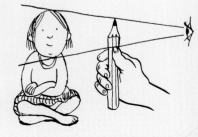

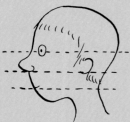

Faces can be different shapes and sizes but there is usually an equal distance between eyes and noses and noses and mouths.

Look out for nose, eye, ear and mouth shapes – you'll be surprised how different they can be.

Portrait...

Portraiture is the art of capturing a likeness of someone – or painting their picture so well that the viewer knows who the subject of the painting is. Portraits can be as detailed and as realistic as a photograph or they can exaggerate the person's features and become a caricature.

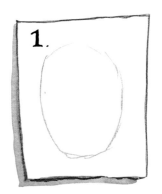

PROJECT

Ask someone to sit and model for you so that you can make a portrait of them. Shine a light on one side of their face to make stronger shadows. This will help you see your model's main features more clearly. Then, using a soft pencil:

1. Sketch the shape of the face.
2. Lightly sketch in the features.
3. Slowly build up the face, adding shadows. Remember not to rub out lines you're not happy with. Instead, keep going over them until you feel they work.

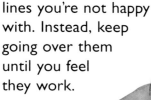

... and caricature

PROJECT

Now I want you to try drawing a caricature. Think about someone you know and decide what their main features are. Perhaps they have a smallish nose and large eyes. Now exaggerate! Make their nose even smaller and their eyes even larger. A caricature should be so distorted or exaggerated that it becomes comical.

Light and shadow

Light and shadow give paintings and drawings shape. You've seen how this works in the portrait project opposite. Shadows can either make things look very heavy or make them float in the air.

PROJECT

Fold a sheet of white card at right angles, then place a small toy on the card. Find a lamp or a torch, then draw or paint the toy and its shadow when you shine your light:

1. Straight on and close to the toy.
2. From above.
3. From two directions.

Now try painting the toy in a warm colour, such as orange, and the shadow in a cold colour, such as blue. Then try a cold colour for the toy and a warm colour for the shadow. Which do you like best?

When drawing shadows, remember that they are usually attached to their owners. If you don't do this, the object that you're drawing will appear to float in the air (see far right).

ART SCHOOL TIPS

People have all kinds of hairstyles and head shapes! Keep a caricature sketch-book to remember them.

*You may have noticed that soft pencils, **charcoal** and pastels can smudge easily. If you want to prevent this, spray your finished drawings with a **fixative**.*

19

1.

2.

3.

20

Use the stained glass window project to experiment further with colours. Make a window using just shades of blue and green. Now make another using reds and oranges.

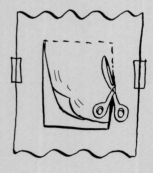

If you want to keep your coloured windows, you could make paper frames for them, as shown above.

Colour workshop

All artists need to understand colour. Colour can be calm or loud, bright or dull. It can even describe moods – we say we feel 'blue' when we mean sad or cold. We 'turn green' if we feel sick or jealous, and if we 'see red' we're angry. Here are five colour projects to get you started.

Kaleidoscope

PROJECT

Collect some coloured see-through sweet wrappers and find an empty cardboard tube (a toilet-roll tube is ideal). Flatten out the wrappers against one end of the tube and hold it up to the light. Move the wrappers around and see how the colours change.

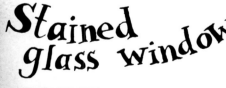

Stained glass window

PROJECT

Tape your sweet wrappers to a window with clear tape. Fold some of the wrappers in half to see how their colours get stronger, then overlap different colours to discover how many new colours you can make. See if you can mix all the colours you see with paint.

Light to dark

PROJECT

Stick a 20 cm strip of double-sided tape onto a sheet of clean, white paper. Find a colour that you like from your paper collection, tear out a small piece about the size of your thumb-nail, then stick it in the centre of the tape. Working out on both sides of the sample, find shades of the same colour ranging from light at one end to dark at the other. Try this with other colour samples.

ART SCHOOL TIPS

Keep a collection of magazines, sweet wrappers and sheets of coloured paper for your projects. They'll be useful when you make collages, too.

Here's how to mix some basic colours to get you started:
Green – blue and yellow
Purple – blue and red
Pink – red and white
Orange – red and yellow
Brown – red, blue and yellow

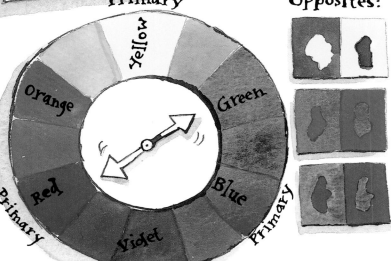

Primary

Yellow

Orange

Green

Primary

Red

Blue

Violet

Primary

Opposites:

21

Colour clock

PROJECT

This colour clock shows the three primary colours – red, yellow and blue. From these, we can mix every other colour. Paint your own colour clock to learn how to mix different colours. The splodges of colour on the left are opposites on the clock. That's why they make your eyes go funny if you stare at them!

Black and white

PROJECT

Look through your paper collection for lots of different samples of white. Also collect samples of white drawing paper, newspaper and wallpaper. Stick all your samples of 'white' on a sheet of paper and notice how many different shades there are. This is because many 'whites' have tiny amounts of other colours mixed with them. Now try the same project with black.

Experiment: Try mixing different colours from the three primary colours. What happens if you add black or white?

ART SCHOOL TIPS

Make a viewer from a piece of card to help you find a good composition for your still life.

22

Sketch lightly with a pencil where you want the objects to go. Look for shapes in the objects, such as circles, triangles and cones. Fill in the shadows with crayons first, then add the paint.

Don't just draw the objects. Remember to look for, and draw, the spaces between the objects, too.

Still Life and Composition

Still life is a really good way to practise what you have learned about colour and to find out about **composition** and shape. A still life is, quite simply, a picture in which the subject is motionless, or still, and has been removed from its natural setting.

PROJECT

Collect some objects with different shapes, colours and textures and place them on a table. Shine a lamp from one side to make interesting shadows. Move the objects around until you find the best arrangement to draw and take time to study the composition before you begin.

ART SCHOOL TIPS

For your still life and other projects you will probably need some kind of drawing board to rest your paper on. You don't need to buy one. Try using a piece of hardboard, a flattened cardboard box or even a tin tray!

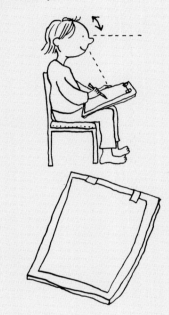

PROJECT

Cut a fruit or vegetable in half and draw it. Try to paint its colour as accurately as you can. Now paint the object again using only shades of blue. Use any blue materials you have, such as paints, crayons or pencils, mixing in black and white to get darker or lighter shades. Then paint the fruit in yellow or green.

Now do some research about still life.

Go and look in the Art History section of your local library and see how many different types of still life you can find. Start by looking for artists such as Vermeer, Picasso and Cézanne then find some examples of your own.

23

Experiment. Use your viewer to look for unusual compositions, too!

Practise drawing without looking at the paper.

*As you draw, try using **watercolour** paints to add splashes of colour over the top of your pencil and crayon lines.*

Reportage

Reportage is the name given to the art of drawing or photographing something as it happens rather than writing about it.

Out of the window

PROJECT

Take a large sheet of paper and some crayons, watercolours and pencils. Sit in front of a window, write the time and date at the top of the page, then cover the whole sheet with drawings from top to bottom. Finally, write the time you finish at the bottom, Now you have a report of all the things that happened out of your window between those times. Real reportage art!

TV drawing

PROJECT

Drawing in front of the television is good reportage practice because you have to draw really quickly to capture anything. Don't waste time rubbing out lines if a drawing doesn't work – start another. Your drawings may not look like much but they are important exercises to help you draw better – a bit like a pianist doing piano scales or a body-builder lifting weights!

Get into the habit of drawing what happens out of your window once a week and notice the changes – not just in what you see, but in your drawing skills, too!

102

25

The artist as explorer

Hundreds of years ago, before the invention of cameras, explorers took artists with them on long voyages to draw the many exciting things they discovered. You don't need to travel many miles by sea or train to be an artist explorer, though. A visit somewhere close to home can be just as exciting, too, as long as you have plenty of imagination.

PROJECT

Explore somewhere. It could be a park, a playground or even your own back garden. It may even be fun to explore a cellar or an attic! Imagine that the place you visit is an island full of strange objects, plants and animals. Imagine, too, that a volcano is going to explode in just three hours and this magical island will sink into the sea forever. Your drawings will be the only surviving record of this wonderful place...

26

ART SCHOOL TIPS

Take a watch on your imaginary travels so you know when your time is up!

It's fun to explore with someone else and compare your work at the end.

Make notes on your drawing to help you remember your imagining

PROJECT

Visit a park, a botanical garden or find some house-plants. Choose a plant you like and draw it:

1. In black and white, using **ink** or crayon and concentrating on texture and shape.

2. In colour.

3. In opposite colours, so that green leaves are red and red flowers green.

4. As an alien plant as big as a house!

ART SCHOOL TIPS

Take the time to really study your subject so that you know what you want to achieve before you begin.

Make notes on your drawings about colours and textures, sounds and smells. If you know them, write down the names of the animals and plants you have drawn, too.

PROJECT

Visit a zoo and make a study of one of the animals there, or study a pet. Make as many drawings of the animal as you can, not just one or two detailed ones. Look carefully at colours, the texture of fur, and so on. Sketches that capture the animal's movement, character or funny habits are important too.

27

Get all your drawing things ready before you set out. Remember to take a plastic bottle of water for mixing paints, and don't forget your lunch!

Remember that if you take red, yellow, blue, black and white paints with you, you can mix almost any colour you need.

Field trip

We're going on a field trip! On a field trip you can learn about making pictures outdoors. Perhaps you can do this project when you go on holiday or on a day trip with your family or friends – but please don't go by yourself!

Really splosh the paint about! You should feel a bit out of breath when you finish!

PROJECT

Find a spot with a view that you want to paint. Carefully unroll your paper (A2 is a good size), spread it out on the ground and put some pebbles on the corners to stop it blowing away. Study the view for a while, then start to draw. Work quickly, swinging your whole arm as you draw and pressing down with your pastels or crayons to get bold, sweeping strokes.

Unless it's raining, leave your drawings out in the air as long as you can to dry. Then roll them loosely in a bin bag until you get back to base. If they are really wet, try rolling them between sheets of newspaper.

ART SCHOOL TIPS

Perspective is a way of drawing distances. A simple example of perspective is that cows far away should look smaller than cows near by.

You don't have to use perspective to do a good drawing. You can make up your own rules. For example, you could:
1. Exaggerate some bits.
2. Make the parts of your picture that you think the most important the biggest!

Take care! Don't go near cliffs or deep water, and never wash dirty brushes in pools or streams because even a little paint can cause pollution.

Take a piece of bubble plastic to sit on in case the weather is cold and wet.

Maps

map on a pebble

Maps are a kind of art, too. They give us information about places in pictures. They can be printed, like road maps, or hand-drawn and faded, like an old treasure map.

Treasure map

PROJECT

Make a treasure map. Hide a coin or some other 'treasure' and draw a map to show someone how to find it. Don't make the map too easy. Try to give interesting clues and remember to use your five senses! You could make a sound map, showing creaky floorboards, or even a smell map of your kitchen cupboard!

START
my bedroom
Open the creaky door
three steps right
follow the sound of soft music
bacon smell
one jump left
to the creaky floorboard
the treasure is under a plantpot

Map in a matchbox

PROJECT

Here's how to make a miniature map that fits into an empty matchbox.

1. Cut out a strip of paper, just wide enough to fit comfortably in the matchbox and about six times longer, then divide the paper into equal sections, Each section should be slightly shorter than the length of the box so that it will fit inside it when folded.

2. Using the lines as a guide, fold the strip into a concertina. Draw a picture and write some instructions in each section, then stick the map into the box.

1.

2.

3.

3. Put the box into its sleeve and you have a brilliant mini-map!

PETSHOP

Cross the road

at the garage

Zoo

left at

get off the bus at the big yellow house

traffic lights

3
2
1

Take bus no 55

ART SCHOOL TIPS

It's fun to think of the different ways your map-reader will recognize their destination. How about a smell of pizza, or loud music from a record shop?

When you make a map, think about using a different viewpoint, such as a bird's eye view or even a frog's eye view!

31

PROJECT

Make a pocket map for a friend showing the best way to get to a shop that you like from where you live or your school. The shop can be any distance – just around the corner or even in a far-off city. Start by giving instructions about how best to travel there – on foot, by bike or perhaps even by plane. Make sure that the most important things on your map are the biggest and the most colourful. Ask yourself whether your friend would be able to use the map easily. You can write words and place names on it if you like.

Mail art

Mail art is making or drawing on envelopes and postcards and posting them, so that the post office's rubber stamps and dates become part of the artwork. It's lots of fun, and it's exciting to think of your mail art travelling great distances through the post!

PROJECT

Collect four or five different-sized envelopes. They don't need to be new. Mail art often looks better if you use old envelopes with used stamps stuck on (although you'll have to add new stamps, too). Draw a picture on each envelope. You can draw anything – a view from your window (especially if you're on holiday), a car, or perhaps a cartoon animal. You could also make one big picture by drawing on two or three different envelopes so that they have to be joined together when they arrive in the post. Or you could try drawing all over an envelope so that it has to be opened out flat to see the whole picture. Don't forget to add a name and address or your mail art will never arrive!

This is the view from my window!

Hi!

ART SCHOOL TIPS

Make your mail art even more interesting by decorating it with lots of 'airmail' or 'fragile' stickers from the post office, or by using special commemorative stamps

Why not post your mail art to yourself!

32

Masks

Masks have been used in magic ceremonies, for dancing, and in plays all over the world for thousands of years. Make some of your own masks and put on a performance for your friends.

PROJECT

Design three masks to show these moods – happy, sad and angry. Use egg boxes and pieces of thick cardboard and decorate them with wool, feathers and pictures torn from magazines.

ART SCHOOL TIPS

Fasten your mask to a stick or tie on a piece of elastic.

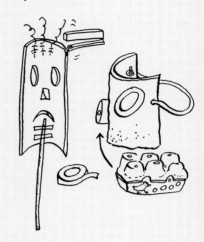

It helps if you paint cardboard with white emulsion before you add other colours.

If you hold a performance indoors, hang up a sheet and shine a spotlight on it to cast dramatic shadows.

Have a look in a library at African and Chinese masks and the work of Picasso who made brilliant masks!

33

Sculpture

Sculpture is the art of shaping and moulding all kinds of materials, such as wood, stone, metal, plastic and wire. Unlike a painting, a sculpture can move, cast shadows, and be touched.

Bust

1.
2.
3.
4.
5.

You will need:
Newspaper ● Tissue box ● Wallpaper paste ● Balloon ● Poster paints

PROJECT

Here's how to make a bust – a sculpture of someone's head and shoulders – out of papier mâché

1. Tear newspaper into strips and soak the strips in wallpaper paste.
2. Blow up a balloon and find an empty tissue box.
3. Cover the base of the balloon with soaked newspaper strips, then join the balloon to the tissue box to make the shoulders.
4. Use scrunched-up pieces of wet newspaper to build the shapes of the eyes, ears and nose and to round out the shoulders.
5. Keep adding layers of newspaper until the balloon is covered. Leave it to dry out thoroughly, then pop the balloon by pushing a pin through the paper. Finally, paint with poster paints or acrylics.

34

Wire sculpture

Wire and chicken netting is good for making sculptures because you can bend and shape it quite easily.

Wire heads

PROJECT

Try making a profile (a side view) of someone from one piece of wire, bent to shape. Tie on wool or raffia for hair. Make an eye from painted cardboard or cut one out of a magazine and hang it in position with string.

Wire fish

PROJECT

Ask an adult to help you cut some chicken wire into a rectangular shape, the length you want your fish to be. Carefully roll it up, as shown, and bend it until you have a good fish shape. You can add a papier mâché skin if you like. Paint it all over with white emulsion and let it dry before you add other colours.

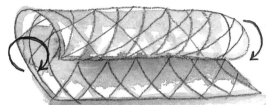
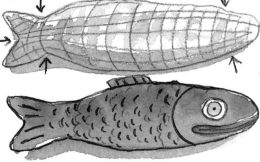

Wire mobile

PROJECT

Make a mobile. Base it on a dream you have had or on one of these themes: Night, Busy Road or Farmyard. Use stiff cardboard for your shapes and attach them to a wire coathanger with thread. Hang the mobile from the ceiling where it will move in a draught.

Draw a simple pattern on a piece of card then glue string over the lines you've drawn. Take rubbings from it when dry.

Always ask permission before you take a rubbing in a church or an old building, and don't press too hard in case you cause any damage.

Frottage

You can get fantastic results when you take rubbings from stone and wood and use them in your art. This is called frottage, a French word meaning rubbing.

PROJECT

1. Find something with raised lettering or pictures on it – perhaps a manhole cover or a gravestone. Lay a sheet of thick paper on top and gently rub a fat wax crayon across the surface.

2. Find a piece of textured wallpaper, rest a clean sheet of paper on top and draw a big, brightly coloured snake. See how the texture of the paper underneath changes the nature of your drawing.

Remember! Frottage can help to improve the character of your drawings so experiment with different textures.

36

Collage

Collage is using things like torn paper, dried pasta shapes, cloth, wool or leaves to create a picture. The more unusual your materials are the better! Collage is another French word, from *coller*, meaning to stick, or glue.

PROJECT

Tear out colours and parts of photographs you like from your collection of magazines then glue them on a sheet of paper to make a picture of an animal or a spaceship. Plan your picture before you begin, sketching the outline and main features with a pencil. Try adding paint on top of your collage for a different effect.

PROJECT

Cut out lots of letters of different sizes and colours from magazines and newspapers. Use the letters to spell your name then glue them to a piece of thick card. Decorate the card with paint and pictures from magazines. Make holes in the top of the card, thread through a piece of string, and hang it on your wall or door.

ART SCHOOL TIPS

Make your collages even more interesting by using shiny sweet wrappers, silver foil or the rubbings you have made.

Try tearing the edges of the paper instead of cutting it and see what a difference it makes to your collage.

Take photographs of your land art so you will be able to remember it and show it to other people. Use a slide film and take your pictures in bright, sunny weather or use a flash to get the best results.

Land art

Land art is when artists work with nature to create a picture or a sculpture. We all know how to make a snowman, a sandcastle or a daisy chain – well that's land art! The beauty of land art is that it doesn't harm nature. It simply melts, washes or blows away.

Try using different drawing tools to make a picture in mud or sand. You could use a big stick, bicycle tyre tracks or even a skateboard.

Think of all the drawings you could make in mud, snow or sand! You could make open-air collages out of fir cones, leaves and twigs, or hang a daisy chain across a tree as an ant bridge!

1.

2.

38

Sand
PROJECT

Here are two sand projects to try if you live near a beach or when you are on holiday:

1. Use bicycle tracks, footprints or a stick to draw a giant picture in the sand. Try to make it so big that it could be seen from space!

2. Go beach-combing and make a strange sea creature from seaweed, sand, shell, pebbles and driftwood.

Snow

PROJECT

If you live in a place which gets plenty of snow, try out these ideas.
1. Build a life-sized snow sculpture of yourself. Use pebbles or other natural materials to make your eyes, nose and mouth.
2. Make a sculpture of an interesting shape. It could be a smooth, rounded shape with huge holes cut into it, a giant cube or a pyramid.

Experiment and find out what happens if you splash a bucket of warm water across a clean snowy surface. Also try a cupful of salt and a spadeful of sand.

ART SCHOOL TIPS

It helps if you use a bucket of warm water and a cloth to smooth icy snow sculptures.

One artist called Andy Goldsworthy went to the Antarctic to carve blocks of ice! Look up his work in an art book in your local library.

Ask someone to take a video of your nature event so you can play it back later. You could also run it if you hold a show (see page 46).

Remember: Always respect nature. Make sure that you never damage any trees or other plants.

Nature event

PROJECT

Next time you are outdoors put on a land art performance with your friends that lasts only a minute. You could float a daisy chain down a stream or toss pebbles in a pool to make ripples in the water. You could throw sycamore seeds into the air or hold two handfuls of dandelion seeds and dance in a circle so that the seeds float away.

It's up to you, but whatever you do, it should be simple, natural and beautiful.

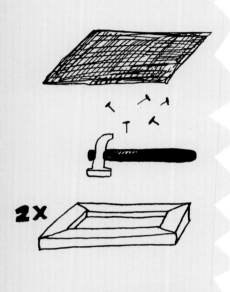

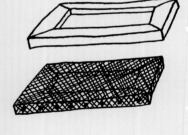

2X

40

Make your own Paper

Making paper is exciting because it never turns out quite like you expect.

PROJECT

To make your own paper you will need:
A pile of scrap paper ● Two buckets ● A large, square washing-up bowl ● A deckle and a mould (you can buy these ready-made from a craft shop ● An old blanket that you can cut up into squares a little larger than your deckle ● Two boards the same size as your washing-up bowl ● A liquidizer ● Cloths (such as dishcloths)

1. Tear your paper into tiny pieces and soak them in a bucket filled with water (just enough to cover them). Leave them for several hours, stirring every now and then.

2. When the paper is soft and squishy, put a handful at a time into a liquidizer and ask an adult to liquidize it for you, or you can mash it with a wooden spoon. Store the pulpy liquid in a clean bucket.

3. Stir a few handfuls of the pulp into a bowl of clean water.

4. Dip your deckle and mould into the bowl. With practice you'll learn how to get an even layer of pulp.

5. Lift gently to let the water drain away, then take off the deckle.

6. Place the net with the pulp side down onto a piece of cloth. It helps if you rock the sheet of pulp onto the cloth. If the pulp tears or breaks up, wash it off in the bowl and start again.

41

8. Separate each cloth and piece of paper and leave the paper in a warm place until dry.

7. Put a new cloth on top and do another. When you have a pile of papers and cloths, put a board and some heavy books on top of them to squeeze out the water. You can stand on them instead if you like – but be careful! You will need to be outdoors or have plenty of old rags handy to mop up the spills.

small flowers

colour

seeds

berries

seeds and leaves

lump of coloured pulp

bits of coloured paper

cut paper

string

feathers

wool

Book work

If you were going to write and illustrate your own printed book, what would it be about? Write some words for a book with 16 pages. Then think about what pictures could go with the words on each page.

Making your first printed book might seem tricky at first but you will soon get the hang of it!

PROJECT

To make your own book you'll need:
Paper ● A stapler ● Scissors ● Paints and pencils ● The use of a photocopier!

1. Fold a large sheet of paper in half, then in half again, then in half once more.
2. Hold it like a book and number each page. (You'll have to part-open some of the pages before you can write the numbers down.)
3. Open out the paper and you'll see that your page numbers are out of order. This is your master plan – a sort of map of how your book must be put together.
4. Now draw your pictures and write your words in the right sections. Remember to write and draw on both sides of your paper.
5. Photocopy one side of the book plan first, then put the copy through again to copy the other side. You'll then have a double-sided copy.

4.

5.

6.

6. Fold the copy carefully like your master plan. Staple it on the spine (the side of the book) and trim the folded edges with scissors.

Now you have your own book! Make as many copies as you like and give them away as presents.

ART SCHOOL TIPS

Sign and number each book on the back. The number on the book below means it's the third copy out of a total of twenty.

Make your books special by printing patterns on the covers with a star-shaped sponge or a potato stamp dipped in paint.

Art history

rt began as a sort of magic charm to help prehistoric hunters catch food. From then on, it has had an amazing history. Browse through the art books in a library and discover it for yourself!

Art has an exciting history full of amazing people... Here are some of my favourites.

Prehistoric artists

Egyptian artists

Jan Van Eyck

Giotto di Bondor

Rembrandt

Leonardo da Vinci

Sir Alfred Hitchcock

Jackson Pollock

Niki Saint Ph

ART SCHOOL TIPS

Make cardboard frames for your big paintings (see page 10) and attach string or fishing line to the corners so you can hang them up.

If you decide to sell some of your work, put the price on a little sticker in one corner. Don't make anything too expensive. It's better to sell more pictures at a low price than nothing at all! If you sell one, put a red sticker on it to show that it's sold. If you don't want to sell something, mark it NFS – 'Not For Sale'.

If you've enjoyed this book, you may like to think about a career as an artist. There are many jobs you could do – you could illustrate books, paint scenery for plays, make sculptures or cartoons, design buildings, magazines, cars or clothes... and many more.

Show

Every art school usually has a show at the end of the year so people can see all the best work its students have done. So now you've finished *Art School*, why not put on your own exhibition?

PROJECT

Hold your show in your bedroom or a garage. Choose a day and a time then send out invitation cards. You may like to prepare some snacks and drinks and play some gentle music. If you've done some projects with friends, invite them to show their work with yours. Try not to be nervous, and good luck!

Glossary

eyelevel

A1, A2, A3
Part of a series of paper sizes ranging from A0 to A10. A1 measures 840 x 592 mm. A2 is half the size of A1, A3 is half the size of A2, and so on.

Acrylic paint
Acrylics come in tubes and can be mixed with water. They dry into a tough, brilliantly coloured waterproof surface and can be used on all sorts of things, from paper and cardboard to wood and plastic.

Brush
Brushes come in all shapes and sizes. Some brushes are made from the tail hairs of a rare weasel-like animal called a sable. Sable brushes are expensive but you can buy much cheaper ones made from nylon which are just as good.

Charcoal
Sticks of burned wood that can be hard or soft and different thicknesses. They are good for drawing.

Composition
How an artist decides to arrange all the objects, people or parts of a view in a painting or drawing.

Crayon
A stick of colour used for drawing, usually made from wax.

Emulsion paint
A paint in which oil and water are combined with a special liquid called an emulsifyer to help them mix.

Fixative
A liquid glue that is sprayed onto a drawing to stop it smudging. If you use fixative, do it outside and get an adult to help as it is bad for your lungs if you breathe it in.

Glue
There are many kinds of glue, and many contain dangerous chemicals. The safest ones to use are water-based gluesticks or PVA — a strong white glue that dries hard and clear like plastic. PVA is good for covering finds in your sketchbook.

Ink
A coloured liquid used for drawing and writing. Some inks are made with water. Others, such as shellac inks, are made with chemicals so they won't smudge if wet.

Masterpiece
A work of art that is thought to be the best piece an artist has ever done. Leonardo's Mona Lisa is a famous masterpiece.

Paper
There are hundreds of types of paper. Go to an art shop and have a look! Some papers are labelled 'acid free' which means they won't fade or change colour with age. **Cartridge paper** is the cheapest, good-quality paper for drawing. **Sugar paper** is cheaply made and comes in different colours but fades in strong sunlight.

Watercolour paper can be expensive because it is usually acid free. It can be rough, medium or smooth in texture and coloured white or cream.

Pastel
A coloured drawing stick that can be chalky or oily depending on whether chalk or oil is used to stick the colour together.

Pencil
The softest pencils are b's and these are the best for drawing. The softer the pencil, the blacker the mark it makes, so a 6b pencil is softer than a 2b and makes a blacker line.

Perspective
A mathematical way of showing distance and **scale** in a painting or drawing. It involves imagining something called a vanishing point. Very simply, you make an object, such as a box, look in **proportion** by imagining lines extending outwards from the box meeting at the same point. It's a complicated subject because there can be many vanishing points in one picture!

Poster paint and powder paint
These paints come ready-mixed with water in squeezy bottles or as coloured powders that you mix with water yourself. They are thick, with the texture of toothpaste, and are great for big, bold paintings and for models and sculptures.

Portrait
A drawing or painting of a person. It can be the whole body or just the face.

Proportion
How big an object or part of an object is compared with another. A tiny head on a large body would be out of proportion!

Scale
Scale is similar to **proportion**. For example, a scale model of a famous ship means that the model has exactly the same proportions all over as the real thing, and a scale model of the ship's captain means that it would be just the right size to fit in the model ship.

Watercolour paint
Paint that is mixed with water to make transparent (see through) layers of colour. For example, to make an orange you don't have to mix red and yellow. You can put a yellow wash, or layer, over a red layer. Also, with watercolours, you do not need to use white because the white of the paper shines through. Watercolours come in little coloured cakes, called pans or half pans, which you keep in a special box or tin.

47

Art SCHOOL
Certificate

I have completed

Art SCHOOL

with excellence

Mick Manning – Tutor

Mick Manning